EXPANDING AMERICA

The Erie Canal

Hex Kleinmartin

Cavendish Square

New York

Published in 2016 by Cavendish Square Publishing, LLC
243 5th Avenue, Suite 136, New York, NY 10016
Copyright © 2016 by Cavendish Square Publishing, LLC

First Edition

Website: cavendishsq.com

This publication represents the opinions and views of the author based on his or her personal experience, knowledge, and
research. The information in this book serves as a general guide only. The author and publisher have used their best efforts in
preparing this book and disclaim liability rising directly or indirectly from the use and application of this book.

CPSIA Compliance Information: Batch #CW16CSQ

All websites were available and accurate when this book was sent to press.

Library of Congress Cataloging-in-Publication Data

Names: Kleinmartin, Hex, author.
Title: The Erie Canal / Hex Kleinmartin.
Description: New York : Cavendish Square Publishing, [2016] | Series:
  Expanding America | Includes bibliographical references and index.
Identifiers: LCCN 2015037124 | ISBN 9781502609663 (library bound) | ISBN
  9781502609670 (ebook)
Subjects: LCSH: Clinton, DeWitt, 1769-1828--Juvenile literature. | Erie Canal
  (N.Y.)--History--Juvenile literature. | New York (State)--Economic
  conditions--19th century--Juvenile literature. | New York
  (State)--History--19th century--Juvenile literature. | United
  States--Territorial expansion--History--Juvenile literature.
Classification: LCC HE396.E6 K54 2016 | DDC 386.4809747--dc23
LC record available at http://lccn.loc.gov/2015037124

Editorial Director: David McNamara
Editors: Andrew Coddington and Kelly Spence
Copy Editor: Rebecca Rohan
Art Director: Jeffrey Talbot
Designers: Amy Greenan and Stephanie Flecha
Senior Production Manager: Jennifer Ryder-Talbot
Production Editor: Renni Johnson
Photo Research: J8 Media

Printed in the United States of America

CONTENTS

A Problem and a Solution

I n modern times, we tend to think of canals as quaint artifacts of the past, good for pleasure boating or fishing. However, at one time, canals could revolutionize trade and industry by transporting people and materials from one place to another.

In the 1800s, the state of New York needed a solution to make the western end of the state, near the Great Lakes, more accessible. Proposals to remedy the problem had been brought up since the 1700s, but the high cost and lack of know-how to turn the plans into reality held up progress. There were no trained engineers in the United States at the time, and boats would have had to travel up and down an elevation of 661 feet (201 meters) between the Hudson River and Lake Erie.

After the War of 1812, the vulnerability of the US frontier in the Great Lakes area became apparent. It also became clear how little control and protection the United States had over its shipping on Lake Ontario, which was controlled by the British. Nowhere else in the United States was there a place where one could travel quickly and easily west of the Appalachian mountain range. President George Washington worried that those far-inland areas might break away from the coast and form their own country, or join with one of the other colonial European powers. However, neither President Jefferson nor President Madison would back funding for a northern canal route, even while other transportation projects farther south were funded by the federal government.

New York would have to solve this problem itself. Although many men helped piece together the Erie Canal, the project would largely depend on DeWitt Clinton, mayor of New York City and state governor, to hold it together and see it through to completion. What follows is a brief account of the tumultuous story of the Erie Canal, filled with twists and turns. Who did what, and how did the pieces fit together to form the Erie Canal?

This painting shows a typical scene on the Erie Canal approximately five years after its completion.

DeWitt Clinton in 1816

CHAPTER ONE

Why Put a Canal in New York?

I n 1789, New York gave up its fourteen-year sovereignty as a British **colony** to become one of the United States under a federal government. For travel into the interior of New York, it was the waterways that helped to settle and develop the state. In 1790, there were about three hundred thousand inhabitants. That number doubled in just ten years, with most of the population living along the Upper Mohawk River Valley, the Genesee River Valley, and around Lake Champlain.

Geography of the Early United States

Why was New York important to the entire United States of the time? The short answer is that New York had a route to the interior parts of what would become US territories in the Midwest, as well as existing original states that were hard to access across the Appalachian Mountains. The Appalachians run from the Canadian province of Newfoundland and Labrador 1,500 miles (2,400 kilometers) southwest to central

An 1827 map of New York

The Erie Canal

Alabama in the United States, and form a travel barrier between the coast and inland areas along its length.

In New York, beyond the Appalachians, a valley houses Lake Champlain and the Hudson River, which cuts right through the mountains near its mouth. Past that, there are more obstacles to westward movement in the Appalachian Plateau. However, the Mohawk River cuts through this and leads right to the nearly level Lake Ontario Plain until it reaches the Niagara **Escarpment**, which holds the other four Great Lakes at a higher altitude. This was the ideal route for the canal to follow; nowhere else along the Atlantic coastline is there terrain that would allow for an easy route to be pursued. This route was also desirable as the Hudson River is **navigable** by oceangoing ships all the way up to the Mohawk River.

Even before the American Revolution, there had been discussions about connecting the Hudson River with Lake Champlain, Lake Ontario, or even Lake Erie. At that time, water travel was much smoother, faster, and required less maintenance than traveling over dirt or even **corduroy roads**.

However, canals were expensive, and height differences were an issue. Leonardo da Vinci had designed the most advanced **lock** for raising or lowering boats, but its design was unchanged from the 1600s, and it was limited in its lifting ability. Also, the United States lacked any trained or certified **civil engineers** who might build canals, let alone improve on them—or be trusted by investors to oversee the construction of any canal at all.

DeWitt Clinton

Of all the people who worked to get a cross-state canal built, DeWitt Clinton would be the man to bolster public support, help to secure financing, and steer the project

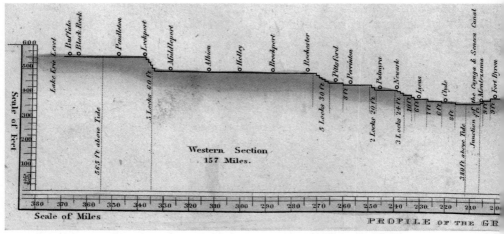

An 1832 profile of the Erie Canal showing the different elevations along its length

through rough political waters—at both the state and federal level.

DeWitt Clinton was born on March 2, 1769. He was later first in his class at Columbia College. Clinton, who was a persuasive public **orator**, served as secretary to his uncle, the state governor, then went on to be active in politics himself. He served as mayor of New York City, a member of the state assembly, both a United States and a state senator, and governor of New York. Clinton pushed for many societal advancements in his political roles, such as creating the New York City public schooling system, city planning, public sanitation, relief for the poor, and organizing the Historical Society of New York.

Clinton backed the canal from the beginning, not just for the benefit of New York City, or even the state. He truly saw it as a means to open up new territories and markets, and to better the United States. For all his temper and abrasive

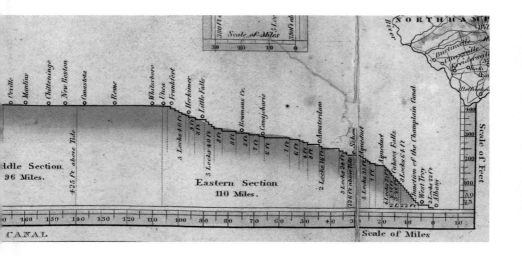

words he might have spoken about his political rivals, he really sought out the betterment of his fellow man. In this case, he was looking to better the lives of people he would likely never meet.

Once the canal became his focus, Clinton threw himself into the project, despite the loss of his first wife and a bad fall that left him with a limp and limited use of one arm. Some would argue that he put far more time into political and social endeavors than he did into his own family's well-being. When he died suddenly in 1828, he had a large state funeral, and there was much public sentiment about the loss. However, his creditors foreclosed on his family, leaving them so destitute that they had no money for Clinton's burial plot. His remains were housed in a friend's family crypt in Albany, New York, until funds could be raised to have them removed and buried in the Clinton family plot, with its own memorial marker, in Brooklyn, New York.

The Onondaga "Fort" (of the Haudenosaunee), based on explorer Samuel de Champlain's diagram

CHAPTER TWO

Settling New York

The first inhabitants of the Erie Canal area were Native Americans of either the Paleo-Indian or Clovis cultures, who lived there around 12,000 to 11,000 BCE. These people hunted large game like the mastodon and elk common in North America at that time. Over the next few thousand years, as the climate warmed and as the glaciers retreated, these people would slowly transition to hunting smaller game like deer and incorporating more plants into their diet.

After 500 CE, the five nations of the **Haudenosaunee** (Iroquois) moved into New York, settling in areas along the Genesee River Valley and through the Mohawk River Valley. Sometime in the 1400s CE, the five nations of the Seneca, Cayuga, Onondaga, Oneida, and Mohawk peoples formed a confederation that still binds them as one group today. The addition of the displaced Tuscarora in 1722 made the confederacy known to colonial Europeans as the Six Nations. Growing fields of maize, beans, and gourds gave them plenty of foodstuffs that could be stockpiled for the winters, while hunting and fishing provided a steady diet of meats. This allowed them to conduct raids and warfare in unprecedented manners upon the peoples predominantly to the north and south of them, and to invest in labor-intensive works like building birchbark canoes to travel on the rivers and lakes of the northeast.

European Settlers

The first non-Native inhabitant of what would later become New York City was a trader named Juan Rodriguez. Rodriguez was born in Santo Domingo, Dominican Republic, to Portuguese and African parents. During the winter of 1613–1614, Rodrigues traveled to the island of Manhattan, where he trapped for pelts and traded with the local Natives. Rodriguez represented the Dutch, who became the next people to colonize the land.

While New York, then called New Amsterdam, would become a Dutch city, and the area around Albany would be first settled by the Dutch, they also spread into the Hudson Valley and the Catskills along the Delaware River's **tributaries**. The Dutch colonial government traded with the then Five Nations, maintaining good relations and giving gifts to the Natives. This helped protect the small farming settlers, mill owners, and manufacturers who lived outside the fort areas. The Dutch and German settlers of New York, who had lived there for a while, disliked the hills and mountains, choosing to settle the flatlands along the rivers. This area's fertile topsoil and lack of large trees made it ideal for agriculture.

The French, who had been settling in Canada, moved into western New York along the Niagara River, leaving garrisons as early as 1679, building a permanent trading post in 1720, and permanently occupying Fort Niagara in

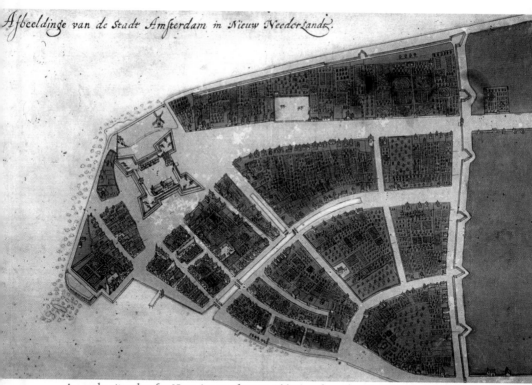

An early city plan for New Amsterdam in 1660 (modern-day New York City)

1726. While there was some amount of settlement outside the fort, it was very small, as there was always a threat of attack from the Seneca nation, which felt that the French were unfairly living on their lands.

In 1664, the British took over the Dutch colony and renamed it for the Duke of York. They tried to ward off French interlopers by building a trading house along Lake Ontario's shore, and secured trading routes with forts there; they built another at what would become Rome, New York, though the main place for trading was still Albany. While more British people moved out of Albany into the Mohawk and Hudson Valleys, they tended to stay near these waterways.

American Settlers and Immigrants

After the Revolutionary War and Sullivan's Campaign, in the 1780s and early 1790s, treaties stripped the Haudenosaunee tribe of most of their territory. Many American and European immigrants flooded the land, settling the newly opened land in central and western New York. Many of the American settlers moving into central New York came from New England, where much of the desirable land had already been claimed and settled. Much of the remaining available land in New England was remote and lacked good infrastructure. It was becoming difficult for New Englanders to find lands from which they could transport their surplus crops or manufactured goods. These Yankee settlers, who were accustomed to living among the hills and mountains of New England, chose to settle the New York uplands, preferring to clear the heavily timbered land rather than build on the expensive and more densely populated lowlands.

Along the canal route, there were communities of Dutch, English, Scottish, Welsh, and German people. With the construction of the canal came immigrants, especially of Irish and Italian descent, who settled in communities along the canal, especially at the **terminus** in Buffalo. These immigrants brought their culture to their new communities, making them unique. For example, the Irish community in Syracuse soaked both potatoes and corn in brine to make salt potatoes and salt corn, dishes that are still served in the area today.

In Buffalo, as the economic and labor **boom** from the canal came to fruition after the canal was finished, the Irish laborers and Italian masons who worked on the canal settled in Buffalo. The population of the city swelled. While the Irish populated the area of the Buffalo River and points

The Buffalo Harbor, where the Erie Canal met with Lake Erie

south, the Italians moved into an area toward the Niagara River. Both areas bordered the canal and gave them access to jobs loading and unloading the **canalboats** and Great Lake freighters.

In Ireland, the Napoleonic Wars and the War of 1812 had just finished. Many Irish soldiers returned to a time of protest, low wages, and high food prices. For those at home, cotton prices in Ireland dropped, the weaving of linen was being slowly mechanized, and cottage industry competition with English manufactured goods was getting harder. Also,

Irish society's weakening of the positions of landowners and farmers aided in producing more unemployed, landless Irish. The canal's expansion corresponded with the height of the Irish Potato Famine, which brought even more Irish to the Erie Canal area.

Italy had been in a depression since the trade routes had changed from the Mediterranean in the late 1600s, and the anticlerical reforms of the 1700s produced discontent and rebellions. After Thomas Jefferson had displayed his affinity for Italian culture, recruiting Italian stonemasons to work on his home at Monticello and Italian musicians for the Marine Band, some Italians felt that things would be better for them in America. Especially for the stonemasons, the prospect of work building bridges and **aqueducts** seemed inviting.

When many of these immigrants arrived, the bank boom was still in force. Some arrived as the loaning bubble burst, and the fiscal situation was even more dire during the

The Erie Canal

The Erie Canal being dug by hand

following depression. With canal work paying $12 a month, this was some of the only work available to newcomers to the country. By 1820, New York was an economic powerhouse. Not only was it the most populous state in the nation, but it also led the nation in exports. Most of the newcomers settled along the Erie Canal route (and that of the Champlain Canal) in northern, central, and western New York, which started to shift the population distribution. Three-fourths of New Yorkers had lived in the Hudson Valley or on the Atlantic Coast; by 1820, that number dwindled to one-quarter. The rest had settled the newer counties in the north and west. At that time, most New York towns were less than forty years old and most residents had come from somewhere else. More than half of New York's current sixty-two counties were incorporated after 1780.

English explorer Henry Hudson

CHAPTER THREE

Exploring the Canal Route

The first European explorer to discover the territory that would become New York was Giovanni de Verrazano, who was leading a 1524 French expedition to find a way through the North American landmass to the Pacific Ocean. While he didn't find one, he did follow the Atlantic coast from somewhere along the coast of South Carolina northward to Nova Scotia before heading back to Europe. While he stayed far enough offshore from the uncharted shallows to miss noting the mouths of the Delaware and Chesapeake Bays, he did spend a day sheltered in the Narrows (between Brooklyn and Staten Island) of what would become New York Bay before sailing farther north.

Without the fabled passage to the Pacific being found, much of North America was being overlooked in favor of finding a way around the continent. Some explorers, like Henry Hudson, were looking for a way around North America, if not through it. On September 10, 1609, his explorations led him to explore New York Bay and, from there, the river that would later bear his name. He was able to take his ship, the *Half Moon*, as far upstream as the current city of Albany. There, he was forced to turn around as the Hudson River became too shallow—only about 7 feet (2 m) deep—for his ship to continue. But even the natural harbor of New York Bay and this navigable river of some 150 miles (241 km) was worth reporting back to his employer, the Dutch East India Company. Hudson's explorations would become the basis for a Dutch claim on what would be known as New Netherland.

Hudson was not the only explorer in the area in 1609, however. The French explorer Samuel de Champlain returned to exploring the interior of northern North America after six years of exploring the coast and building up the settlements of Acadia and Quebec in what would become French Canada. Champlain had, along with François Gravé in 1603, explored several tributary rivers of the St. Lawrence, making it as far upstream as the modern city of Montreal, where they were stopped by the Lachine Rapids. There, they encountered Natives who could speak with their interpreter and found out about three "great lakes" farther upstream along the St. Lawrence. Champlain hoped that one of these was actually the Pacific Ocean. On their trip back down the St. Lawrence, they explored the Richelieu River and met other Native Americans who told them of a river to the south that ran to the coast of a great salt sea.

Inland into New York

When Champlain returned in 1609, he went back to the Richelieu River and made his way down to the lake that now bears his name. After going as far south as he could along the lake, he and two other Frenchmen started to explore to the south on foot. He made it to Ticonderoga, a few months before Hudson's ship would be turning around at Albany just over 80 miles (129 km) to the south. It was here that he used his arquebus, an early European firearm, to help some of the Canadian Native groups defeat some Mohawks of the Haudenosaunee (Iroquois) Confederacy, an act that would have long-term ramifications for the relations of French Canadians with the Native Americans of New York.

In 1613, Champlain explored across Ontario, along the Ottawa River to Allumette Lake by canoe, working to befriend the local Natives and convince them to allow French trappers and fur-traders to work in the area. He continued along this route in 1615, starting from Allumette Lake and making his way farther along the Ottawa River to Lake Huron, then coming back through Ontario to the eastern end of Lake Ontario. Here he accompanied some friendly Huron into what would become New York to wage war on the Haudenosaunee. Encountering either the Oneida or Onondaga near what would be Syracuse, Champlain was wounded in battle and had to be carried away by the retreating Huron to the northern shores of the St. Lawrence River.

The British and French in New York

When Britain acquired New Amsterdam from the Dutch in 1664, France was concerned about having an aggressive rival so close. The French feared Britain's easy access to the Great Lakes along the Mohawk River. Much of this rivalry came out in more aggressive trading ventures and diplomacy based in trade agreements.

However, there was plenty happening on the eastern side of the state as well. In 1685, James Rosebloom, a trader based in Albany, hired some French deserters to lead him into the French fur-trapping/trading area of

Forts and Trading Posts

By 1614, the Dutch were making inroads as well, most of them via trading rather than direct exploring. Fort Nassau was constructed at Albany to protect Dutch trading interests; it allowed the Dutch to form strong trading bonds with the local Mahicans (Mohicans) and later the Mohawks. As the Natives they traded with showed off their spoils, other Natives from farther away came to Fort Nassau. They made pacts and gave information about the lands and the people around them. In this way, the Dutch gained general information without the danger of traveling and secured some amount of protection (or at least warning of attack) from their trading partners nearby.

However, Fort Nassau was located on Castle Island (now Westerlo Island) and was damaged repeatedly by spring floods caused by runoff from melting snow in the Adirondack, Green, and Taconic mountain ranges. In 1617, Fort Nassau was moved to a higher point near the **confluence** of Normans Kill Creek and the Hudson River, but it was destroyed the following year by more of the river's spring flooding. Fort Nassau was left abandoned in 1618 and replaced by Fort Orange in 1623, which was built

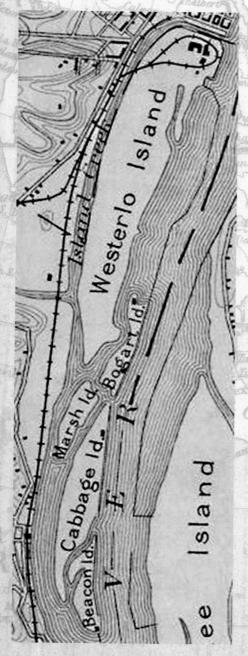

Westerlo Island, originally called Castle Island by the Dutch, was the original site of Fort Nassau in 1614.

about 5 miles (8 km) south of the confluence of the Mohawk and Hudson Rivers.

Some Dutch traders, however, did make trips out into the Haudenosaunee lands, like the trader Harmen Meyndertsz van den Bogaert. Over the winter of 1634–1635, he traveled to several Haudenosaunee "castles," as he called the palisaded villages of the Mohawk and Oneida tribes he visited. In addition to giving a fairly detailed account of the villages, he also noted the French trade goods, and he entreated the Dutch at Fort Orange to trade more favorably with the Haudenosaunee to compete with the French for loyalty.

But while the Dutch were passively exploring, the

Frenchmen were more active. Even as the French focus pushed farther west along the Great Lakes and through Canada, French Jesuit missionaries were out exploring and attempting to convert the Native Americans to Christianity.

Haudenosaunee history, and archaeological evidence, indicates that European fur traders had certainly been through their lands as early as 1635, but these records often did not recount their travels with great accuracy. Likely, some wanted to appear greater or more impressive than their competitors, and others may just have wanted to protect some lucrative trading partners from being poached by another trader.

In 1679, the French established their first post on the New York side of the mouth of the Niagara River and named it Fort Conti. The explorer and trader René-Robert Cavelier, Sieur de La Salle, was able to obtain permission from the Iroquois to build the fort and use the Niagara **portage**. As there was no way to portage a real sailing ship over the Niagara Escarpment from Lake Ontario to Lake Erie, he was determined to build one on the Niagara River above Niagara Falls. La Salle's party of explorers and ship carpenters were the first Europeans clearly documented to have explored the Niagara River and view the falls. Built over the previous winter, La Salle's vessel, the *Griffon*, was launched on the

The Erie Canal

upper Niagara River in the spring of 1679. It was from here that he would explore the Great Lakes and make his way down the Mississippi River to the Gulf of Mexico in 1682.

Over the winter of 1678–1679, La Salle established Fort Conti to support his shipbuilding project. He had found a high bluff at the mouth of the Niagara River whose lack of trees made it a good place to build a fortified storehouse. Fort Conti was in a good position to communicate with La Salle's base at Fort Frontenac, located on the eastern end of Lake Ontario, as the mouth of the Niagara River provided a safe harbor for large sailing ships. Fort Conti's storehouse was used to supply La Salle's men working above the falls, although all the supplies needed had to be carried by hand or back up over the Niagara Escarpment, which rises approximately 200 feet (61 m) in about 0.25 miles (0.4 km), and the distance from Fort Conti to the building site was about 15 miles (24 km). Fort Conti was abandoned, however, after it accidentally caught fire and burned shortly after La Salle left the fort.

Michigan, where he would trade with the Ottawa Natives. This trip, however, would take him across all five of the Haudenosaunee lands and through some of the areas from Albany to Tonawanda that the Erie Canal would follow 150 years later. Another Dutch trader and interpreter for the British, Arnout Viele, traveled through southern-central New York and down into the Ohio Valley to establish trade with the Shawnee in what would become Indiana and Kentucky. He even persuaded some of the Shawnee to come back with him to Albany to help transport the furs. As much as these were explorations, they were not systematic surveys; they were forays, but they brought back valuable information, nonetheless.

Fort Conti's successor, Fort Denonville (1687–1688), was equally short-lived. The new fort was established in 1687 by the governor of New France, Jacques-Rene de Brisay, Marquis de Denonville. Denonville organized a military expedition to eliminate the Iroquois, who posed a threat to New France. In addition, Denonville hoped to weaken the growing British influence in Iroquois territory.

Denonville lead the expedition himself. He first set his sights on the Seneca, the westernmost of the Haudenosaunee nations. His army attacked Seneca villages in the Genesee River Valley (south of modern-day Rochester) with limited success. Denonville then turned west toward the Niagara River, where he established a fort. In July 1687, Denonville's soldiers built a stockade, and the fort was named Fort Denonville. When Denonville departed for Montreal shortly after, he placed Captain Pierre de Troyes in command of the fort's garrison, which numbered one hundred.

Denonville had hoped his assault would frighten the Seneca; instead, like kicking a hornet's nest, the attack had the opposite effect. The Seneca saw the fort as an encroachment on their territory. Denonville's soldiers frequently spotted Seneca warriors lingering near their isolated camp. Although Denonville had hoped this fort would subdue the Seneca and secure the entrance to Lake Erie, manning it became a death sentence for many of the French soldiers stationed there. While the Seneca did not attack directly, disease and starvation soon had a dramatic effect on the inhabitants of the fort. When Lake Ontario thawed in spring 1688, only twelve of the one hundred soldiers were still alive.

In spite of this disaster, Denonville assigned a new garrison to Fort Denonville, but the post was only occupied until September 1688, and then abandoned. Isolation and the hostile Haudenosaunee had rendered it untenable and had proved a formidable obstacle to French efforts to establish a presence at Niagara. More than three decades would pass before they would maintain a military force at Niagara.

One of the things that the French required to ensure their position at Niagara was a more substantial fortification, not to say that they were not trying to maintain control. One way they were doing this was through trade, as with Louis-Thomas Chabert de Joncaire, a French agent for New France, who had run a trading post at the foot of the Niagara Escarpment and portage in Lewiston, New York, since 1720. While watching and exerting some control over the portage route, Joncaire reported back to the governor of New France that the Seneca would allow a new post, as long as it was not a masonry fort.

In 1725, the French asked the Haudenosaunee for permission to build a new stone trading house in Niagara. A Native delegation assembled at Onondaga, where they agreed to listen to the proposal. The French called the building a "House of Peace" where Frenchmen and Natives alike could exchange furs and other goods. Although representatives of the Seneca Nation raised issue with the proposal, citing the recent French attacks on their villages and the continued encroachment on their land, the Five Nations granted permission. The French went to work immediately despite continued Seneca protest. However, unknown to the Natives, this "House of Peace" was to be used for more than just trading.

The French left the design of the trading post to Gaspard-Joseph Chaussegros de Lery. De Lery designed a two-story turreted stone house, which would be surrounded by a wooden stockade. Such defensive stockades were common to most European trading posts in North America. While de Lery's house appeared to look like a typical trading post, it was also designed to function as a fort. It featured all the facilities needed to repel a Native assault and house a garrison, including quarters for soldiers and officers, a storeroom, a covered well, and more. The "trading post" was so well fortified that American soldiers in the War of 1812 placed cannons in the attic and fired on British troops across the Niagara River. The "French Castle," as it is known, still stands today.

In 1724, William Burnet, the captain-general and governor of New York, sent Cadwallader Colden, the surveyor general, westward from Albany to report back on the composition of the territory (and the activities of the French and the Native Americans) in New York and beyond. Colden was not one to shirk his duties, and he traveled as far west as the Mississippi River. His report, titled "A Memorial Concerning the Furr-Trade in the Province of New York," provided detailed descriptions, including topography and waterways, of the areas he visited. In his report, he compared the French route up the St. Lawrence River, which represented awkward travel during the winter months, to the waterways of New York, in terms of how easily they could be navigated. He shared that he could get from Albany to Lake Erie by canoe with only short portages to continue to the next waterway. He also reported on the economics of the fur trade of the west and how best the British might capitalize upon it, though at that time there was no easy way to do so. The report emphasized how the rivers of New York were more calm and manageable, and the geography was more flat or gently sloped, than that of French Canada, and did so without the 18 to 20 foot (5 to 6 m) tidal variations that the St. Lawrence River was subject to. In bolstering this case, Colden speaks of the Hudson as being not only fairly straight but also "very free from sand banks, as well as rocks; so that the vessels always sail as well by night as by day, and have the advantage of the tide upwards as well as downwards."

By 1727, traders using Colden's information had charted a route from Albany, along the Mohawk River, along Wood Creek to Oneida Lake, and then along the outflow river to Oswego at Lake Ontario. The British colonial government decided to establish a trading house at Oswego. By 1729, the British had built a fort at the trading house to protect this trade, and another, Fort Stanwix, would be built at the headwaters of the Mohawk River near the Wood Creek carry in the current town of Rome, New York.

Americans Explore

During the American War for Independence, the British and the Native allies organized raids out of Fort Niagara, which threatened the output of New York and Pennsylvania farms whose crops went to feed the army. Two of these raids in particular—one in the Wyoming Valley of Pennsylvania and the other in Cherry Valley, New York—were so damaging to the war effort that the Continental Congress authorized

The "French Castle" at Old Fort Niagara, the first stone building in western New York

General John Sullivan

military action into the unknown New York frontier. In 1779, George Washington ordered General John Sullivan and his army to punish the Haudenosaunee for aiding the British. The Haudenosaunee were ill prepared to fight a colonial army on the open field. Sullivan's troops recorded little resistance as the Natives withdrew, leaving Sullivan's men to burn crops and villages. Sullivan's army stopped their advance at the Genesse River, just 80 miles (129 km) from Fort Niagara. Although Sullivan had the opportunity to attack the British there, he decided against it. The weather had started to turn, and Sullivan did not have sufficient provisions to besiege a British fort, let alone make it through a harsh Western New York winter. Instead, Sullivan chose to winter in well-supplied Pennsylvania. The Haudenosaunee who had survived the battles with Sullivan faced starvation during the winter of 1779–1780. Many moved to the areas around Fort Niagara in order to survive.

Elkanah Watson in 1782

CHAPTER FOUR

People and Events That Led to the Erie Canal

O ne prominent person strongly associated with the fledgling United States is George Washington. He was one of the first US officials to be concerned with an endeavor like the Erie Canal. Because some of the original thirteen colonies held land on both sides of the Appalachian Mountains, Washington was worried that the settlers on the Western side might break away from the United States and form their own nation. Or, even worse, they might join up with Britain, France, or Spain, who still had colonial presences on the continent, and limit the future expansion of the unallied United States.

There had been some attempts in the 1770s to connect the Potomac River, which runs through modern-day West

Virginia, Maryland, Virginia, and Washington, DC, with areas east of the mountains. However, these ideas lost investors and interest as the many hurdles that lay ahead became apparent. The rut-filled dirt roads or "Indian paths" of the Native Americans that served as the infrastructure of the United States were unpredictable in quality, and insufficient for trade and industry to be built on. Wild animals were also a concern. It was obvious that a different solution was needed.

In 1784, Washington appealed to his friend Thomas Jefferson for advice. Jefferson supported enhancing the Potomac through Virginia, though he recognized that the Hudson–Albany–Mohawk Valley route already existed, and that the Potomac route "is still to be opened." After traveling with New York's first governor, George Clinton, from New York City, through Albany to Lake Erie, Washington referred to New York as "the seat of empire."

Washington started in 1784 and worked until 1788 to promote and fund his Patowmack [sic] Canal project despite legal and engineering issues between two states, nonpaying investors, swift currents, rocks, and flooding. While the canal was open by 1802, it turned out it was only really useful for bringing goods downstream. The waterway was too shallow for any of the early steamboats, and the current was too fast for push-poles or dragging the boats along with ropes or chains. The Patowmack Company, established to lead the canal project, would eventually go bankrupt in 1810.

Canals in New York

Even with this founding father's failure, others would try. The first attempt at a canal along the western route from Albany was a piece of Wood Creek, which ran westward out of the same swampy area that the Mohawk River ran eastward from. Both Wood Creek and the Mohawk River had many **meanders** in this area, and in 1730, some unnamed trapper(s) had invested the time and energy to dig a channel between the closest areas of a meander to create "the neck digged through," which cut off several hours of travel time along the route. While not much of an improvement in the overall travel of the area, this was the first documented use of manpower to improve waterway travel, and arguably the first canal in the United States.

Another attempt was made by Christopher Colles, an Irish immigrant, mathematician, and mechanic who had been in charge of engineering for improving the navigation on the River Shannon in Ireland. In 1776, Colles designed a system of pipes made from hollow logs to transport water for New York City's water system. In 1784, he put forth a proposal to the New York State legislature arguing that the rewards for improving navigation on the Mohawk River would be tremendous. In his proposal, Colles pointed out that, as the ground between the Upper Mohawk River and Wood Creek was perfectly level, this was an ideal site to create a channel to the west. In May 1785, the legislature funded Colles to undertake an on-site evaluation of the work needed to clear obstructions along the Mohawk River up to its headwaters near Lake Ontario. However, while his 1786 report discussed the opportunities in glowing terms, "and for extending the same, if practicable, to Lake Erie," Colles was unable to gain investor support, forcing him to abandon the project.

Another man who pushed for the improvement of waterways was Gouverneur Morris, a noted politician and patriot. In 1777, Morris worked to help bolster sentiment and morale in the Continental Army at General Schuyler's headquarters, when he spoke of the "useful arts in our country … that at no very distant day, the waters of the great inland seas, would, by the aid of man, break through their barriers and mingle with the Hudson." In 1780, Morris would say in a letter to a friend, "Shall I lead your astonishment to the verge of incredulity? I will: know then, that one-tenth of the expense borne by Britain in the last campaign, would enable ships to sail from London through Hudson's river into Lake Erie." While it would take time, Morris's words would come to fruition, but not without hard work.

The man who would undertake the first phase of that work would be Elkanah Watson, a man who had started off as an indentured servant. Later, he gained famous friends, including Benjamin Franklin, John Adams, the Marquis de Lafayette, Alexander Hamilton, Aaron Burr, James Watt, and Edmund Burke. Watson, for all of his social climbing, was enamored by canals in Europe. He toured many, such as the Bridgewater Canal, which had elevated sections as well as others that went down into a coal mine, and had revolutionized travel and commerce in England in the 1760s. Watson had even been a guest of George Washington in 1785, and had become infused with "canal mania" in their talks about how to solve the Appalachian problem. Later, he would insist that he was the first person to ever conceive of the idea of the Erie Canal, though others felt they had a better claim to the idea. However, it is true that in a 1788 trip to examine the swampy headwaters of the Mohawk, Watson observed, "the citizens of the state of New York have it within their power, by a grand stroke of policy, to divert the future trade of Lake Ontario and the great lakes above, from Alexandria and Quebec, to Albany and New York."

While Watson was full of enthusiasm, in order to convince the legislature and investors, he needed documentation and the accounts of other credible people to back his arguments and plans. Toward this end, in 1791, he took a few of his influential friends westward from

Albany on a six-week-long examination of the waterways. The trip followed the proposed canal route and ended at Geneva, on Seneca Lake. This, of course, is not the whole length of the Erie Canal, and Watson would admit that "We should not have considered [a canal linking Lake Erie and the Hudson River] much more extravagant to have suggested the possibility of a canal to the moon." But even with the limitation of Watson's aims, he did assess, in reasonable terms, the viability of a canal linking the Mohawk to Lake Oneida and thus to Lake Ontario at the very least. Watson's report also included comments on the climate and economies of the areas they passed through, noting things like salt deposits near Syracuse and the abundant crops of farmland along the canal's proposed route.

Western Inland Lock Navigation Company

Enlisting the aid of state senator Phillip Schuyler, a war hero and wealthy landowner, and writing letters and reports for various New York and Albany newspapers, Watson saw the support for his idea grow. Later that year, the legislature passed a bill that had been jointly drafted by Schuyler and Governor George Clinton, called the "Mohawk Improvement Bill," the first of several bills to set the stage. The legislature then chartered the Western Inland Lock Navigation Company to develop the Mohawk to Lake Ontario, and the Finger Lakes (if possible). With Schuyler as president and Watson on the board of directors, the pair quickly began finding investors and starting work.

Most of what the Western Company set out to do was what Washington's Potowmack Company had done on the Potomac: namely, to improve the navigability of the river, not build a canal. While locks would be used in places where rapids or waterfalls might threaten passage, for the most part, the route would follow the existing rivers' courses rather than creating a more direct route. Some of this was possibly for the best, as there were no trained engineers available to oversee the work, forcing Schuyler to name himself the chief engineer, although gout and politics kept him away most of the time.

The labor force of approximately four hundred men would clear the Mohawk River of debris, sandbars, and stones. Dams were built to raise water levels where things could not be removed, and the men worked to build locks mostly on their own. This meant that the monumental task of building step-locks to carry ships around the Cohoes Falls and other declines where the river drops more than 200 feet (60.7 m) in only 16 miles (25.7 km) between Schenectady and Albany was out of the question. The real work started at Schenectady and went upstream from there. The largest improvements were a series of five locks to bypass Little Falls, where the river falls over 40 feet (12.2 m) in just three-quarters of a mile (1.2 km), and two more locks and 2 miles (3.2 km) of true canal near Rome to connect the Mohawk River to Wood Creek.

This endeavor, leaving a portage between Schenectady and Albany and following the twists and turns of the Mohawk and Wood Creek, changed central New York within a few short years. The boats that had been used on these waterways to transport goods and people were bateaux, which were small, able to be portaged, and could only carry less than 2 tons (1.8 metric tons) of cargo. Now, boatmen could use Durham boats, which were flat-bottomed, often 60 feet (18.3 m) long and 8 feet (2.4 m) wide, and capable of carrying 20 tons (18.1 t) of dense cargo, or up to 150 barrels of other cargo. These boats could be rowed and steered by nearly 20-foot-long

(6-meter-long) oars, or by sails set on masts when the wind was favorable.

This increased cargo capacity, and the relative ease with which a six-man crew could operate these huge boats upstream, made water travel along this route profitable. According to a 1789 Western Company report, the cost of transportation of a ton of cargo from Albany to Geneva fell from $100 per ton to just $32 per ton. From Albany to Niagara Falls, the cost was cut in half. The report also commented on the various types of raw and manufactured goods coming to Albany, and the imported and manufactured goods going back upstream for trade.

While the economies of towns, villages, and farms along the canal's route blossomed, the Western Company itself faltered. Many of the subscribers never paid up their full amounts, so the accounts were never filled. The locks needed constant maintenance, and even the toll **revenues** could not keep up with expenses. Despite this, the locks and dams proved how well such a waterway could work, even while people were hesitant to invest their own money in such an endeavor.

The idea for the Erie Canal was alive and well. In a series of conversations between 1803 and 1805, Governeur Morris spoke to New York State Surveyor General Simeon De Witt (DeWitt Clinton's first cousin) about tapping Lake Erie to make an "artificial river, directly across the country to the Hudson River." However, De Witt thought Morris's concept of the canal, a constant inclined plane, was more a romantic fantasy than a workable proposal. James Geddes, a salt entrepreneur, judge, and assistant in the surveyor general's office, also discussed the concept with Morris. Geddes later relayed the idea in conversations with a local flour merchant named Jesse Hawley who, within a few years, would become the Erie Canal's most vocal proponent in the press.

Jefferson's Suggestion

While plans for the canal were still being bandied about, President Jefferson actually thought out the process into action. In his second inaugural address of 1805, Jefferson announced that the treasury had a surplus of around $3 million, and that the money should be "applied in time of peace to rivers, canals, roads, arts, manufactures, education, and other great objects within each state." For a second time, in 1807, in his annual message to Congress he recommended spending the federal government's surplus funds on "internal improvements."

One of the New Yorkers that this resonated with was Robert Fulton, who is best known for inventing the steamboat, but who had also written a book on small canals in 1796. He examined the recommendations that the Secretary of the Treasury, Albert Gallatin, had made for spending the federal surplus, and he went from the theoretical gains of building canals for the country's economy to the practical steps that would be needed to make it happen. He estimated that the construction of a canal would cost around $15,000 per mile, but by reducing the manpower to one horse-tender and one steersman per boat for 25 tons (22.7 t), rather than the multiple teams of horses, drivers, and carts needed to transport by road, "the merchandize which can bear the expense of carriage on our present roads to … any … distance of 300 miles, and which for that distance pays 100 dollars a ton, could be boated on canals *ten thousand miles for that sum.*"

With this information available to New Yorkers, they moved quickly to try and secure some of this funding, as the Western Company's shortfalls had led to financial support from the state legislature. Here was an opportunity to gain federal funding for a venture, rather than state capital.

In February 1808, Assemblyman Joshua Forman, from Onondaga County, proposed a resolution for a canal to join the Atlantic to "western waters" after a long discussion with another assemblyman, Benjamin Wright, who had done most of the surveying for the Western Company in the 1790s. This discussion had been about "true" canals, and not the "navigable improvements" that the Western Company had undertaken. There was an understanding that, while it would be a much harder task to undertake, transport along the canal would be steady in either direction (not being subject to currents), and would foster immense growth along its course, helping the endeavor to quickly pay for itself.

While he was initially jeered at, Forman brought up examples like the immensely profitable Bridgewater Canal in England and France's Canal du Midi, which had the world's first canal tunnel; their benefits; and the mere (over) estimated cost of the Erie Canal at only $10 million. Finally, in April, the resolution was passed, and it allotted $600 to cover the costs of surveying a suitable route by the surveyor general, with a report and maps produced to submit to President Jefferson. Surveyor General DeWitt entrusted the surveying to James Geddes but instructed him to make the survey based on a two-canal system, where boats would skirt the coast of Lake Ontario from Oswego to wherever the second canal would make its way over the Niagara Escarpment to reach Lake Erie. However, Geddes was from the area where Syracuse is today and decided, on his own time and expense, to survey on from Oneida Lake to the Genesee River near Rochester.

While Geddes undertook his survey, DeWitt was negotiating a canal route with the Holland Land Company representatives who owned most of the land between Rochester and Buffalo that the canal might pass through. The resident agent in the area was Joseph Ellicott, who had

DeWitt Clinton (left), along with Simeon DeWitt and several others, received a commission from the New York State Legislature to survey possible routes for the canal.

been surveying most of his life and had a stake in the sale of the holdings of the Holland Land Company. As such, Ellicott had the trust of his superior in making decisions and disbursing funds. While Ellicott did not supply DeWitt with a full survey of the whole area, he did provide a map and description of his recommended route through the area, as well as conditions for crossing the land and how the company might contribute both land and money to the project if these conditions were met.

Thus, later in 1808, DeWitt had all the information needed to submit the proposal to the federal government in Washington, which he did—only to get no response. After months of silence from Washington, in January of 1809, Forman secured a copy of the documentation from DeWitt. He then traveled to obtain an appointment with President Jefferson to inquire about the status of the proposal, and to submit it himself, if it had been "mislaid." It turns out that Jefferson had just not responded, and Forman was, perhaps due to the failure of the Patowmack Company, subject to a frustrated response: "… here is a canal of a few miles, projected by General Washington, which, if completed, would render this a fine commercial city, which has languished for many years because of the small sum of 200,000 dollars necessary to complete it, cannot be obtained from the general government, the state government, or from individuals—and you talk of making a canal of 350 miles through the wilderness—it is little short of madness to think of it at this day." Despite this response from the president, Forman did not back down. Instead, as he left, his parting words were that the "state of New York would never rest until [the Erie Canal] was accomplished." Forman remained true to his word, making it his business to make the canal happen.

But before this could happen, the economy changed, as Jefferson took action against policies the warring French and English were taking toward American trade. Jefferson felt that neither the French nor the English would be able to survive long without the raw materials that the United States provided, so he issued the Embargo Act of 1807. This act made it illegal for Americans to export goods but allowed imports from foreign countries. The end result was that European nations ignored the loss of American goods for the most part, and struggling American farmers, especially those in western New York, started smuggling their goods to Canada, which was an accepting market that could then export them freely to Europe.

After President Madison succeeded Jefferson, he tried to reverse the failing policy with his Non-Intercourse Act of 1809, which would allow Americans to export their goods but made it illegal to import European goods. Again, it didn't have any effect on the warring nations and their treatment of American ships and sailors. But, like the Embargo Act, this new act caused economic turmoil in the United States and made it hard to garner support for the New York legislature to fund the canal project. It was not until 1810 that the canal's cause was again taken up, this time by Thomas Eddy, one of the first directors and the acting treasurer of the failing Western Company. After yet another year with the Western Company being unable to pay any dividends to their stockholders, and looking to the state for funding, Eddy tried to convince his fellow directors to extend the company's canalworks 75 miles (121 km) farther west to the Seneca River. There, the terrain was more level and wouldn't have the maintenance costs that the tempestuous Mohawk River incurred.

But the directors of the Western Company had no funds to undertake any further development, and no real support from investors who had not seen any appreciable dividends on their investment in years. So Eddy approached Jonas Platt, a state senator and the leader of the Federalist party, to try and gain support for a canal. While Platt was initially against the idea of the canal as a private venture, he felt he could back the concept if it could instead be a state agent not solely out for profit. And while Eddy was only looking to get the canal to the Seneca River, once convinced, Platt saw no reason to stop there, though the endeavor would have to be politically sound in addition to being well-engineered.

The Canal Commission

After hours of discussion, Platt and Eddy put together a "canal commission" with the political and engineering backbone that they felt would see the proposal through. Beside themselves, James Geddes was selected, as he had already surveyed the area and was a recognized expert in his field. He was to be accompanied by his friend and fellow surveyor Benjamin Wright, who was a also a friend of Forman. There were three other Federalists selected: Governeur Morris; Stephen Van Renssalaer, the owner of the most property in New York who had been on Watson's 1791 trip; and William North, a respected war veteran.

While these members were certainly rich and powerful, the politics of the day would never have let this pass. The Federalists of the time wanted rule of a few educated and wealthy landowners, while the Republicans of the day wanted a more democratic system, where each citizen had equal say in the government no matter how much land or money they had. Platt, realizing this, selected three Republicans to balance things out. The first was DeWitt Clinton, then mayor of New York City. The other two Republicans were the Surveyor General Simeon De Witt and Peter Porter, a United States congressman from western New York who owned a large amount of property and some businesses there. Porter had previously attempted to pass a resolution for a canal from Lake Ontario to Lake Erie as a means to enhance his portaging business's profits after Jefferson's announcement, but it had gone nowhere.

While the members of the canal commission would name Morris as senior member, in many ways it was Clinton who actually made things happen. Once set upon a task or a concept of betterment for the people that he represented, he was very hard to dissuade. With this lineup, the legislation approved the proposal in 1810. In July of that year, the commission, by various means, set out to see the canal route for themselves. It took them fifty-three days to travel from Albany to Buffalo. They had to write their report and try to get it approved by the legislature as quickly as possible. Clinton thought that they should present as a united group, all supporting the report, but Morris, as senior member and as someone who had drafted not only New York's constitution but also much of the US Constitution, felt he should be the one to draft the report. No one argued.

However, Morris still held onto his idea of a smooth, inclined plane, taking the waters of Lake Erie and letting them flow, with a mild downhill current, into the Hudson River. The other members protested that this would entail building **causeways**, some more than 100 feet (30.5 m) above ground level for miles, and in other places tunnels or great cuts, as the terrain was full of hills and valleys. Morris wouldn't budge, and the commission needed to submit a report, so Clinton got all the others to sign on to Morris's plan, though Porter held out the longest.

Clinton hoped that the report would be seen as "hypothetical" and as a "suggestion" of things yet to come when it was finally submitted to the legislators, and that the legislators would review it with common sense. With the unanimous backing of the commission, it was assured that any canal endeavor would be solely overland, that it would be an artificial canal for its entirety, and that since the federal government would not pay for any of it, it would be a work undertaken by public financing of about $5 million, owned and controlled by New York. Though there were some doubtful individuals, mostly in western New York, and some debate in the state legislature after the report was published in 1811, it took only a month for the first of a series of bills dealing with the canal to pass. This bill **appropriated** $15,000 for the commissioners to work out financing, purchase the interests of the Western Company, and to make another attempt at approaching the United States Congress for some of Jefferson's promised funds.

New York Goes It Alone

Morris and Clinton went to Washington, DC, to present their case. However, President Madison argued that the Constitution didn't really allow for it, and his reluctant message to Congress about improving the transportation infrastructure of the nation gave no help to the canal project. Most of the representatives were watching out for the interests of their own states, rather than the nation as a whole. Morris and Clinton were surprised at how even states bordering New York refused to help, emphasizing that New York and the canal commission would be on their own. When Clinton reported this in 1812, he also reported that Morris's "inclined plane" was just one of several methods that could be used. And, due to additional surveys, they thought the cost for the entire project would be $6 million, and the expected toll revenues would be $600,000 per year (at a toll of $2.50 per ton). This would cover the interest due on a $10 million loan at a rate of 6 percent. These estimates, based on numbers worked out by Gallatin and Fulton using actual **customhouse** data from the Hudson River, made a strong impact on the legislature. Despite arguing over the expenditure of public funds and how the canal would be a tax drain on those whose lands were not within a day's carriage ride from it, a special session of the legislature would authorize the commission to purchase the rights to the Western Company, negotiate for funds in the name of New York, pursue surveys, and complete the final canal design.

Unfortunately, within a month of this law being enacted, the War of 1812 with Great Britain was declared in June, stalling progress on the canal. In addition to wartime problems, like securing European financial backing, western New York and the Great Lakes were on the battlefront. The canal also faced other political problems. Clinton had been fighting against Tammany Hall, the mayor of New York City, and his "**bucktail**" politicians who worked against anything that Clinton was for, including the canal.

The War of 1812 was mostly a series of losses in combat for the Americans, with the notable exception of naval battles, where American **frigates**, like the *Constitution*, were more maneuverable and had greater firepower than the British ships. This was also the case on the Great Lakes, where there were few warships present on either side. The Americans built six new ships at Erie, Pennsylvania, in the first year, though the cannon and shot had to be transported by road from the Atlantic coast to ready the ships for battle. Commodore Oliver Perry would use these ships, plus several small ships from Buffalo, to beat the British naval forces on September 10, 1813, where his report of his victory would give us the phrase, "We have met the enemy and they are ours."

Despite the war and the turmoil in New York, the canal commissioners kept working, submitting a new report in 1814. This report confirmed their earlier estimates more firmly and outlined a suggested scale for tolls, complete with comparisons of shipping costs from other places around the country. However, the bucktails and landowners farther from the canal, and the financial pinch of the war, caused pushback in the legislature. A clause was added to one of the existing canal bills that stripped the commission of the ability to arrange funding for the canal. Relegated to a powerless advisory committee, the commission did not even submit a report in 1815. Adding insult to injury, Clinton's political rivals had him replaced as mayor of New York City. His term as lieutenant governor having run out in 1813, Clinton was now entirely out of office. Disheartened about the future of the canal due to petty politics, he did what he could to continue promoting the project.

As Clinton wrote and spoke, he displayed how tenuous the United States' grasp on the western frontier was due to poor road conditions and the number of men and horses pulled from the war effort for transport. He cited the example of Commodore Perry's cannons. General James Tallmadge's report of 1816 indicated that a cannon could be produced at an eastern factory for only about $400, but that it cost from $1,500 to $2,000 to ship to Lake Erie. Likewise,

The Erie Canal

Commodore Oliver Perry's naval forces secure the upper Great Lakes by defeating the British during the War of 1812.

it took weeks to ship it there over "roads so abominable as to make cannon balls cost a dollar a pound." Clinton also discussed the importance of local markets and having the ability to move American goods around the new nation, via better canals and roadways.

While Clinton was making his case to the public, Platt and Eddy were scheming to get things going in the legislature again. Eddy again went to Clinton, who, buoyed by the support, renewed his efforts. Clinton hosted and publicized a **symposium** in the City Hotel in New York City with many speakers, including himself, lecturing on the canal and its benefits against its low cost. The meeting in December 1815 attracted more people than the hall could hold. After a small booklet was printed of all the lectures (almost all of them penned by Clinton), Eddy and some of his colleagues hosted more meetings in the city. They also traveled to twenty-five other cities in the state, not only to spread the information about the canal, but also to collect signatures on a petition in support for the canal. They collected nearly one hundred thousand signatures, although the total population of the state was only about one million people, and at that time only men could vote.

In 1816, the state assembly voted in favor of the canal 91-18. However, in the state senate, Martin Van Buren, a rival of Clinton's, argued to block the canal project until it had more detailed plans, and the senate voted down the canal 19-6. As part of this vote, they appropriated $20,000 to pay for the commission to do more research before they would vote again and appointed five members to replace the original seven. There was more disappointment at the federal level, when Representatives John Calhoun of South Carolina and Henry Clay of Kentucky worked out a bill to sponsor New York's canal project with $90,000 per year for twenty years. Seen as a way to bind the divided Northern and Southern states, this bill passed in Congress and barely passed the Senate, giving the canal commission hope. That is, until President Madison vetoed the bill, on the same day as signing an appropriation for $100,000 of roadwork in the Cumberland Gap, a project that Jefferson had started in 1805.

While Clinton was incensed at this move, there was little cause for uproar. He was one of the newly appointed canal commissioners, along with Ellicott, Stephen Van Rensselaer, Myron Holley, and Samuel Young. This rid the group of some of the idealists and put in more practical thinkers, like Holley, an assemblyman from the Finger Lakes region; Young, who had already written a survey of canals in England and Holland; and Van Rensselaer, whose interest in science and engineering would cause him to found the Rensselaer Polytechnic Institute in Troy. The new commission got to work on the details, knowing that Van Buren and his faction were still working against them.

The first order of business was to divide the canal into three sections: from Lake Erie to the Seneca River, from the Seneca River to Rome, and from Rome to Albany. Construction would start on the middle section as it would need no locks, helping to give the engineers and construction crews experience before tackling the tougher end sections. The commission also worked on funding, proposing a possible tax on all properties within 25 miles (40 km) of the canal (as they would get the most benefit from the canal), though this was never imposed. Another proposition was that there could be taxes on the salt from near Syracuse, and on passengers coming from steamboats in the Hudson, as well as on imported auction goods.

While there were no accredited engineers in the United States at the time, the commission chose Geddes as engineer of the western section; Wright as engineer of the middle section; and Charles Broadhead, another surveyor with engineering tendencies, for the eastern section. A fledgling engineer named Canvass White would later join the engineers after he spent his own time and money trekking along 2,000 miles (3,219 km) of British canalways on foot to examine their construction techniques up close.

In addition to the Erie Canal, or the Great Western Canal as it was sometimes called, the commission was tasked with constructing another canal from Albany to Lake Champlain. This would take only one surveying trip at what Clinton estimated as a cost of $24,000. All of the information they had amassed on both canals was put into a report in early 1817, estimating the cost of the Erie Canal at $4.9 million, and the Champlain Canal at $900,000. While these were staggering prices for the time, the task at hand was one that had never been tackled before, covering 363 miles (584 km) and having locks to take the boats up and down an altitude of 661 feet (201 m). And in the report, the commission recommended that the first work would be limited to the middle section, which was relatively level and would cost only $1.5 million.

Now, it was up to the legislature. The debates were heated, but the state assembly carried the bill 51-40. However, the assembly had been pro-canal before, and the vote still had to be carried in the senate, where Van Buren still held power. But Clinton had just won the governor's seat with 97 percent of the vote and Van Buren was a master politician. In a surprising turn, he gave an impassioned speech citing many petitions from voters and favorable personal communication with the new governor, voting squarely for the canal. It would pass the senate vote 18-9, though this would not actually be the last hurdle.

At the time, the New York legislature included a Council of Revision, which could veto any legislation that it deemed inappropriate and could only be overruled by a two-thirds majority of the assembly and senate, much like a presidential veto. This council had five members: the governor, the chancellor, and the three justices of the State Supreme Court. While only one of these was a direct enemy of the canal, two others had problems with committing to such a project without more sound public opinion behind it and thought that the project gave the commissioners arbitrary powers over the rights of the people. While Clinton and the others were for the canal, it looked like it would fail in this council, 3-2.

Things changed on a "chance encounter" when Daniel Tompkins, the vice president of the United States and the ex-governor of New York, stopped in "just to visit." Finding out that they were arguing about the canal, Tompkins addressed the Council, telling them in "all confidence" that the War of 1812 wasn't really over; it was only in truce and there would be another war with Britain within two years.

The resources of New York should not be wasted on the canal, but on preparing for war. At this, Chancellor Kent, one of the holdouts on the Council of Revision, changed his mind, stating, "If we must have war, or have a canal, I am in favor of the canal, and I vote for this bill." As such, plans for the canal moved ahead.

Digging the Ditch Starts

The first stretch of construction began just outside of Rome, New York. This section, like the others through the middle section, was being dug by contracted teams of locals, overseen by the surveyor/engineers, and occasionally assisted by paid laborers. The commissioners felt that they would get more dependable labor and more enthusiastic response to the canal by having those who lived nearby take part and get paid. But it was not an easy task, clearing land to a 60-foot (18 m) width in the midst of dense forests, and digging a ditch 4 feet (1.2 m) deep and 40 feet (12 m) wide along the length of the section. All of this labor was completed with horses, oxen, plows, shovels, wheelbarrows, and the hands of many men. One technological advancement that would help was a new product from the E.I. Du Pont de Nemours Company called "blasting powder," which was a more powerful explosive than black powder, but not as powerful as dynamite would be when it was discovered. In addition to all this digging, bridges needed to be built—as low as possible—to facilitate moving farm animals, equipment, and material from one side of the canal to the other as the "ditch" would split nearly two-thirds of the width of the state into north and south sections.

By the end of 1817, 58 miles (93 km) of canal were being worked on, about a thousand men were being paid through around fifty contracts, and 15 miles (24 km) of canal were fully operational. The regular pay for a workman was $12 a month (often with meals included), paid from the contract holder who, in turn, got paid by the commission. These rates were good compensation for losing a day's work on a farm, and the work was steady and mostly occurred at times when farms did not need intensive labor, making the income a bonus.

With many people along the canal route seeing this as an incentive, by the summer of 1818, contracts had been signed for the length of the whole canal except in places where the engineers would have to build locks, bridges, or aqueducts. Over that same time, with over 4,000 men and 1,500 horses involved in the project, the commissioners were publicly projecting that the middle section would be complete by the fall of 1819, only two years after the initial excavation had started.

The year 1819 was not as cooperative, bringing terrible weather in the winter and spring and more mosquitoes and other biting bugs than usual. These not only annoyed the workers now toiling in and near the swampy areas west of Syracuse, but they also spread **malaria** and other illnesses. At least one thousand laborers fell sick with "fevers," and even Clinton's wife, Maria, died from a fever while trying to escape the insects on Staten Island by staying with friends in Westchester County.

Despite all this, by late summer, the middle section of the canal was complete enough so that the section could be filled with water, which was accomplished for the Rome to Utica section on October 22. As the **sluicegates** were opened in Rome, the water flowed out toward Utica, and people all along the canal length came to watch. A canalboat, the *Chief Engineer*, was prepared for Wright, and at 61 feet (18.6 m) long, 7.5 feet (2.3 m) wide, and a draft of only 14 inches (35.6 centimeters), was pulled along by a horse and 60 feet (18 m) of rope. Traveling at what would

The Erie Canal crosses over the Mohawk River at the Upper Mohawk Aqueduct in Rexford.

become the standard speed of 4 miles (6.4 km) an hour, the commissioners made the 16-mile (25.7 km) trip in four hours, a military band aboard playing to the cheers of people along the banks. The following morning in Utica, amidst a celebration, the commissioners boarded the *Chief Engineer* for their return trip to Rome. The canal was about to start producing revenue.

Engineering the Canal

In 1820, work began on the Utica to Albany section of the canal. While the middle section was relatively flat and had no locks, the western section started with a series of thirteen locks to compensate for land drops of 105 feet (32 m) over 8 miles (12.9 km). Wright and White had spent many hours searching for an alternate route, but it turned out that the Mohawk Valley was the best way despite its twists, turns,

The Depression and the Canal

As much as New York was taking care of itself in terms of building the canal, the national situation would still come into play. What had started as a downturn in economic activity in 1818 would become the crash of 1819, the first economic depression the United States would suffer at the hands of mismanaged banks and investors. While this would hit the ordinary citizens of New York hard, the canal would prove to be a saving grace, and the crash would actually help the canal.

In the wake of the War of 1812, many small banks had ended up printing more money than they actually had gold or silver to back, which caused a boom and **inflation**. To try and curb this, Congress reinstated the Bank of the United States, which Jefferson had abolished, to try and curb the power banks and bank shareholders held in politics. Congress hoped that by having the Bank of the United States handling the major funds of the government, and by imposing rules on how much money it could issue (not to exceed $35 million), and how much gold it had to hold against that (at least $7 million), that other small banks would fall in line and curb their issuing of currency.

Instead, with poor leadership in the form of Captain William Jones as its president, the Bank of the United States joined in with the smaller banks, overissuing currency (lending $41 million and having $23 million outstanding) and not keeping the reserve funds needed to secure its debts (only $2.5 million gold). This freewheeling of the banks came to a halt in the fall of 1818 when a payment of $3 million in gold to France for the Louisiana Purchase of 1803 came due, and the Bank of the United States had only $2 million of gold in its vault.

Forced to borrow funds from London to pay the debt, the bank directors installed Langdon Cheves as bank president. To try and rectify the bank's fiscal situation, he drastically cut new lending, and within two years the outstanding deposits were reduced to $10 million; by 1821, there was $8 million in gold and silver in the vaults of the bank. But this came at a high cost. The Bank of the United States called in loans, both to smaller banks and to larger investors, many of whom were forced to **liquidate** their assets or call in loans of their own to meet these payments. These calls affected farmers and small business owners across the nation, and there was simply less money available in the economy as banks shored themselves up, forcing many into poverty and to become landless due to losing farms and homesteads that they had put up as collateral.

In the midst of this, the solidity of the Erie Canal project, which was already generating toll and **tariff** revenues and was backed by the state, was one of the safest loans a bank could afford to make. In this reduced economic climate, banks were competing for good loans, and the interest rate dropped from 6 percent to under 5 percent, decreasing the actual cost of the canal to the state, while at the same time, increasing the labor pool available and making the pay of $12/month a living wage for men with a family. The areas around the canal had plenty of cashflow and experienced less poverty than much of the rest of the country.

There was no worry that the canal would not be funded, as in 1818 Clinton had helped to start a bank that catered to modestly increasing the deposits of widows and workmen by investing in safe loans; by 1821, it held almost 30 percent of the canal's outstanding **bonds**. Also by 1821, there were over nine thousand men at work on the canal and every interest payment to investors had been made in full and on time. With the middle section totally completed since the fall of 1820, generating toll revenue that exceeded projections, the Erie Canal was one of the best investments to make in those troubled times.

and drops. The area at Little Falls was one of the most taxing areas for these self-taught and observant engineers, where whitewater rapids plunge down over 40 feet (12.1 m) through a narrow **gorge** in less than half a mile.

While work at Little Falls, with its locks and aqueducts, was continuing in 1821, the canal from Little Falls eastward to Schenectady was filled with water. Work on this section had often required the use of blasting powder to excavate the canal path and **towpath** areas from the solid rock of the cliff walls. In other places, the canal had to be elevated far above the Mohawk River, with the whole stretch requiring thirteen locks to make it a smooth transition. But if that or the work at Little Falls seemed daunting, it was the work at Cohoes Falls that would be the biggest challenge of the eastern section. There, twenty-seven locks were needed and much of the canal had to be elevated to zigzag back and forth across the steep hillsides as the canal rose over 200 feet (60.1 m) in 16 miles (25.7 km). This undertaking involved two notable aqueducts, the northbound at almost 750 feet (228.6 m) long and 300 feet (91.4 m) tall, and the southbound at almost 1,200 feet (365.8 m) long, all so that canalboats could safely pass over the raging Mohawk River. At the falls themselves, the route was blasted out of the cliff walls, with Wright fearing that they may have to build the canal through a tunnel if things did not work out well.

But the dramatic crossing of the Mohawk, even with the aqueducts and blasting, was more cost-effective than expected with the previous design, which had included having the canal only on the south side of the Mohawk River. When the eastern section was complete in 1824, the commission's report stated that they expected the entire canal to be running within the next year. They admitted that if they had started at the Hudson and worked west (instead

A 1906 panoramic photograph of Rochester, showing both the Genesee River and the Erie Canal aqueduct crossing over it

of starting with the middle section), the canal project may have been delayed by as much as one hundred years. And yet it was done, just seven years after the first excavations had started. Now, the focus turned toward the west.

In this region, the first hurdle would be crossing the Irondequoit Valley. The slopes were too steep for locks down one side and back up the other, and the soil was too soft for a bridging aqueduct. Geddes was forced to deal with a massive **embankment** from one side of the valley to the other, taking the canal in some places six stories higher than the valley floor. But this caused another problem, in that the Irondequoit was a navigable waterway that needed to flow and be accessible to boats. To solve the problem, Geddes designed a massive **culvert** 25 feet (7.6 m) high, 30 feet (9.1 m) wide, and 100 feet (30.5 m) long so that boats would be able to cross under the canal. Even with this building technique, the soft earth was a problem, necessitating the sinking of almost one thousand log **pilings** down into the ground to more-stable dirt below, providing a solid foundation to build on.

But the Irondequoit Valley was far from the worst of the western section's engineering dilemmas. At Rochester,

an aqueduct was needed to carry the canal over the swift-flowing Genesee River next to the Genesee Falls, a job first undertaken by William Britton in 1821. He had just finished building the Auburn state prison and brought nearly thirty convicts to work on the job, as a means to increase his profits. However, he decided that he needed more convicts, that the convicts needed guarding, and that the local, red Medina sandstone was unsuitable for the task. When Britton died that spring, a new contract was drawn up and the aqueduct was completed in 1823, shored up with stronger **limestone** from farther east, but eleven months behind schedule.

The last of the engineering feats was to raise the canal up and over the steep Niagara Escarpment, between Rochester and Buffalo. This entailed raising the canal up about 60 feet (18.3 m) in less than 0.1 miles (6.16 km). This posed a couple of problems. For one, the rise could not be handled by one or two large locks, because each gate had to be able to be operated by one individual. Using several smaller locks, however, was not possible, because the rise was too abrupt and did not allow for the long stretches of water necessary. The solution came from one of the canal's staff engineers, Nathan Roberts, who designed a system of a flight of five locks. Each of these locks had 12 feet (3.7 m) of lift, rather than the 9 feet (2.7 m) of all the other locks on the canal. To speed up travel through these locks, he designed two parallel flights, one for traffic up (west) and the other for traffic down (east). However, there was yet another dimension to the engineering involved, as the locks would get the canal to the desired height, but the bedrock of the escarpment went up yet another 10 to 15 feet (3 m to 4.6 m) above the viable water level of the canal. The only cost-effective solution was to simply dig and blast out the bedrock until it was lowered enough for the canal to run through. This meant cutting a trench 10 miles (16 km) long and as much as 30 feet (9.1 m) deep.

The rock was so tough that it broke standard hand drills, so specially hardened bits had to be procured to drill holes for the blasting powder to be applied. Lighting the fuse was not seen as a man's job, but that of a boy—"powder monkeys," as they were called, were thought to be able to run faster over the jagged and uneven surface than a grown man. The men would clear the jagged rubble using a specialized **derrick** that lowered buckets into the canal cut to be filled, then lifted and swung them over the edge to be dumped above. Then the empty buckets would be lowered again. Additionally, towpaths had to be cut into the rock at about 15 to 20 feet (4.6 m to 6.1 m) above the canal where the ground rose above the water level. Both the locks and the blasting were started in 1823. The blasting was finished in late 1824, with the locks being completed in June 1825. As the remainder of the canal followed the existing slow-flowing Tonawanda Creek to the Niagara River, water could now flow.

While these engineering feats were being accomplished, there was a dramatic, political, power struggle going on between Peter Porter and the city fathers of Buffalo over where the canal would end. Porter's land holdings caused him to lobby for ending the canal at the village of Black Rock, just 3 miles (6.4 km) north of Buffalo along the Niagara River, where a natural outcropping of flat, black limestone provided a solid dock at a place where the fast-flowing river split around two islands. Porter promoted how this protected harbor would be the logical endpoint of the canal, which was already coming upstream from Tonawanda Creek. However, he neglected to point out the strength of the current at the head of the Niagara River where it flowed out of Lake Erie. Even sailing ships could not leave the harbor without the services of the "horn breeze," a team of oxen pulling the ship up the river to Lake Erie. The village of Buffalo, on the other hand, had the slow-flowing, meandering Buffalo River mouth and no currents from Lake Erie, but no protected harbor. While the fight would change the end point of the canal back and forth between these two locations for nearly a decade, by 1825 it was decided that a breakwater and harbor would be constructed in Buffalo. This would be the terminus of the Erie Canal.

After Clinton had left the governor's office in 1823, his political career was faltering. He had been voted out of office through bucktail machinations, and his choice of making Buffalo the terminus of the canal made him an enemy in Porter's eyes. In April 1824, his role as lead commissioner on the canal commission was Clinton's only political position. The bucktails who were in power in the state senate and assembly came up with a scheme to finally remove Clinton from the entire political scene. During the last moments of the regular legislative session, Senator Bowman introduced a resolution to remove Clinton from the canal commission, which passed without debate 24-3. Immediately afterward, the senate adjourned. As the assembly repeated the issue, after the resolution was

"The Wedding of the Waters" in New York Harbor, as DeWitt Clinton pours water from Lake Erie into the Atlantic Ocean.

The Erie Canal

read to the floor, three assemblymen stood up to speak for Clinton. One even asked what, in fact, Clinton was guilty of, but no answer was forthcoming. Only the vote passing the resolution 64-34 and the adjournment of the assembly followed.

This transaction came as a surprise to the people of the state and backfired on the bucktails, as they found that Clinton now had the "sympathies of the People." Thousands of protestors and mass meetings brought their concerns over the actions of the government to Albany and New York City. Clinton was overwhelmingly chosen for the nomination as candidate for governor, an election that he would win with a safe margin. In addition, his supporters came into power in both the assembly and senate, giving Clinton the support of nearly 75 percent of the state legislature.

In 1824, Clinton became governor, and the nearly finished Erie Canal was already productive, with its proceeds already exceeding interest payments by $400,000. The canal was finished in October 1825, and the canal commissioners and many others took a lavish celebratory trip from Buffalo to New York City. The celebration started on October 26, with a long parade of canalboats loaded with not only many animals that existed in New York, but also casks of water from Lake Erie. Over the next eight days, the canalboat parade stopped at towns, cities, and villages along the canal for festivals and speeches. The journey culminated with a steamboat pulling Clinton's canalboat into New York Harbor, where a ceremony was undertaken to "wed the waters," as Clinton emptied water from one of the Lake Erie casks (as well as water from the Nile, Ganges, Thames, Mississippi, and other major rivers around the world) into the Atlantic waters. The Erie Canal was officially open for business.

Modern lock doors on the Erie Canal
(now the New York State Barge Canal)

CHAPTER FIVE

Rewards of Clinton's Work

I n looking at the long-term effects of the Erie Canal, it is easy to get caught up in the technical achievements of the project. This sort of efficient improvisation by untrained workers is what would later be called "Yankee Ingenuity," but at that time it was just "making the work go faster with less back-breaking labor."

New Technologies

Because of the work needed to fell trees and remove stumps along the canal's path, workers developed new labor-saving devices for these jobs. One cable and pulley system could, with one end of the cable around the upper trunk of the tree, convert the pulling strength of one man into enough force to bring the truck to the ground. This either snapped the trunk near the base or pulled up the roots as it went. The traditional method of stump removal was to dig down far enough to tie a rope under some of the bigger roots on one side of the stump, then pull with your horses or oxen on the other side to roll the stump up and out of place. However, for some of

This 1825 lithograph shows a method used to remove rock from the Erie Canal above the escarpment near Lockport.

the massive trees along the canal route, this was not enough power to bring up a stump.

Instead, some of the canal workers developed a massive three-wheeled axle to do the job. The axle was around 30 feet (9.1 m) long and nearly 2 feet (0.61 m) in diameter. The two outer wheels were about 16 feet (4.9 m) in diameter and turned freely on the axle, while the third wheel in the middle was fixed to the axle and had a diameter of 14 feet (4.3 m). The device could be hauled into place with a horse or oxen, positioned just over or near to the stump. Next, the outer wheels were braced, and a chain was attached to the stump and then wound around the axle. A heavy rope was then wrapped a number of times around the middle wheel, then pulled by a team of horses or oxen. The force produced was tremendous, and rather than having a team

The Erie Canal

of men spend a day attempting to dig and pry out a stump, or using expensive blasting powder that would still leave roots to be removed, seven men with a team of four horses using one of these devices could remove between thirty and forty stumps per day.

Another new technology developed while building the canal was the excavation method. Originally, men used spades and loaded dirt into wheelbarrows and carted it away. But in looking for easier and better ways to remove the soil, the Erie Canal builders hit upon the idea of using horse-drawn plows with sharpened iron blades fixed to the plow edges. These would not only loosen the packed earth, but also slice through roots, making it easy for men with spades and shovels to load the dirt into carts and sledges that would be dragged away by teams of horses to be dumped elsewhere. To keep the horses from packing down the already-plowed earth, or the earth that would later be plowed to be removed, the men led the teams along the towpath areas, an action that ended up packing down the edge walls of the canal much more securely than traditional methods. This helped to strengthen the edge walls against breakage or water loss from leakage, saving water in the dry seasons and money in overall maintenance costs.

Another local invention that later aided development in other areas of the United States was "Chittenango cement," a **hydraulic cement** that could be used in the canal locks and aqueducts without wearing away and causing leaks that would require shutting down a section of canal for repairs. Created using the natural limestone found in New York, this material would be analyzed and used for decades to come when waterproof building materials were needed, not just along the Erie Canal. In 1819, Canvass White began the first natural cement factory, in Chittenango. His product proved so successful that White quickly expanded operations wherever he found limestone. The area around Rosendale (near Kingston on the Hudson) proved to have the best rocks around, which were unearthed when the Delaware and Hudson Canal was being dug in 1825. The cement turned out to be so good, the term "Rosendale cement" became interchangeable with hydraulic cement, and was used all over Manhattan and the New York Harbor, even as the base for the Statue of Liberty. It was also used in other cities and harbors up and down the Atlantic coast.

The canal workers also devised the derricks for clearing away the debris in the "big cut" at Lockport. These would not only be used to clear away debris from deep railroad cuts throughout the country in years to come, but also in mining operations. Another great invention was the **weighlock**, which could weigh a boat to find out how much cargo it had to determine the tariff it should pay. Weighlocks used Archimedes's water-displacement method and only required a boat to stop in the lock to work, making them fast, efficient, and profitable.

Nathan Roberts's engineering of the dual flights of taller locks at Lockport, along with proving that a canal could be cut into bedrock, laid the foundation for a viable transoceanic canal in Panama. Combined with what American engineers had learned about channeling and controlling water by undertaking and successfully completing the Erie Canal, endeavors like the Panama Canal became possible. Even the biggest of oceangoing ships at that time could be lifted and lowered to cross Panama's mountains from the Atlantic to the Pacific and back.

In fact, during and after the construction of the Erie Canal, patent applications for new tools and technologies skyrocketed, from about two hundred per year in the years from 1810 to 1825 to more than seven hundred per year in 1835. These patents would be for items like James Dart's

The Weighlock Building on Erie Boulevard East & Montgomery Street in Syracuse

1834 steam-powered grain elevator, which could in only a couple of hours unload a grain barge that would have taken more than eighteen men a whole day's work. Such open exchange of ideas, new situations, and opportunities, and potential for easy mobility of people along the canal, set up the area to lead the nation in new patents per capita in almost all economic sectors. Even as New England began to lead the country in manufacturing, the canal corridor maintained a close second for the rest of the country.

Taming the West

Beyond these technologies is something even more important for the growth of the United States. Goods could now be shipped from the Great Lakes to the Atlantic more quickly, more safely, and more inexpensively than they could before. The economy of the villages, towns, and cities along the canal's route boomed. New York City became the biggest and most prosperous harbor in the United States, eclipsing New Orleans. As Buffalo grew and became a city, its harbor's size grew, too. By 1900, it was ranked the eighth biggest city and the fourth busiest harbor in the United States, and that included the time that it spent iced over in the winters.

Along the Erie Canal came not only the goods, but also the people who would settle most of the Midwest. Since Washington had been concerned with states having territory on the west side of the Appalachian Mountains, Jefferson

The Erie Canal at the top of the Lockport Locks, around 1855

The Erie Canal

had expanded the country with the Louisiana Purchase, adding 828,000 square miles (2,144,510 square kilometers) of land to the west of the Mississippi River. Before the Erie Canal, many settlers in that area came through French Canada, along the St. Lawrence River, or up the Mississippi River from New Orleans. After 1826, more and more of these settlers took advantage of the cheap cost of transport on the Erie Canal, then traveled farther across the Great Lakes to places like Chicago. There, a short portage, and later a locked canal, could take them to rivers connecting to the Mississippi and its tributaries. This opened up huge amounts of land, allowing settlers to get the supplies they needed and to transport crops and manufactured goods to other American markets and foreign markets through ports like New York. In the years following the canal's completion in 1825, the cost of transporting goods between the Midwest and New York City fell dramatically, in some cases by 95 percent. With the Erie Canal being the only truly accessible way to transport goods to and from the areas west of the Appalachian Mountains, Washington's dream of uniting the lands came true, just not in Virginia as he had imagined.

Societal Impacts

Some people did claim that the Erie Canal brought about negative impacts. One of the largest that attracted public attention was the behavior of the canalboat crews. As the canalboats made their way along the canal, they were towed by horses and mules guided by young men, often orphans. Working on a canalboat crew was backbreaking work, and many men who joined were rough, rowdy types who lacked education. Such young men made up more than a quarter of the workers on the Erie Canal, and they were notorious for their coarse language and behavior. In 1839, Daniel

The original westbound series of five locks at Lockport still exist and are used as an overflow spillway alongside the single modern lock that is used today.

Wandell told the Canal Board that "the Boys who Drive the horses I think may safely say that these boys are the most profane beings that now exists on the face of the hole erth without exception."

Residents in upstate New York were concerned at the behavior of the canalboat crews when they were not at work. They drank, they gambled, and they fought. The

The Erie Canal

offenses most prosecuted by police included intoxication, fighting, creating nuisances, vandalism, and soliciting sex. The Canal Board noted that boatmen often did not respect the property of others. Even those canal workers paid by the state, such as lock tenders, were considered rude, ill-mannered, and dull as a result of the "simple labors" they undertook repetitively which did not stimulate their minds.

Other canal protesters included religious locals who lived along the route. Some complained that the operation of canalboats violated the sanctity of the Sabbath, a holy day of rest that for Christians takes place on Sundays. They petitioned to prohibit boat travel on Sundays. Others, however, disagreed. They argued that if boat crews were given Sundays off, they would be more likely to disturb whatever town they were passing through, drinking, swearing, gambling, and fighting. This argument won out, and canalboats continued to operate on Sundays.

In the 1900s, the railroads overtook the Erie Canal, but its presence has undeniably shaped New York. One lasting impact is in demographics, where even today 80 percent of the state's population outside of New York City still lives within 25 miles (40.2 km) of the Erie Canal. In 1992, the canal ceased its commercial operations. Today, it is used purely for recreation.

Chronology

1524   Verrazano discovers New York Harbor.

1609   Hudson sails up the Hudson River to Albany. Champlain travels south from the St. Lawrence River to Ticonderoga.

1614   Dutch establish Fort Nassau on the Hudson River.

1623   Dutch establish Fort Orange at Albany.

1634   Van Den Bogaert travels in Haudenosaunee lands.

1664   British acquire New York from the Dutch.

1679   French establish Fort Conti at the mouth of the Niagara River. La Salle builds and sails the *Griffon* on the upper Great Lakes.

1685   Trader Roseblum travels through New York to Michigan.

1720   Joncaire establishes a French trading post at Lewiston.

1724   Colden makes detailed survey of New York (west of Albany).

1726 French establish a permanent presence at Fort Niagara.

1727 British establish a trading house and fort at Oswego.

1776 British colonies in North America declare independence from Great Britain, form the United States. War of Independence begins.

1779 Sullivan's Army marches against Haudenosaunee in central/western New York.

1792 Western Inland Lock Navigation Company incorporated to open the Mohawk River to navigation from the Hudson to Ontario and Seneca Lakes.

1803 President Jefferson negotiates the Louisiana Purchase, adding 828,000 square miles (2,144,510 sq km) of land to United States' territory.

1805 President Jefferson's address suggests that there are federal funds in surplus to be used for infrastructure works.

1807 Jesse Hawley begins to write essays about the feasibility of an overland canal between the Hudson and Lake Erie.

1808 New York state legislature votes to authorize a survey of possible canal routes from the Hudson.

1810 Appointment of first New York canal commissioners

1811 The commissioners request financial aid from the federal government and neighboring states, which is refused.

1812 War of 1812 begins with Britain. Industrial development booms in northeastern states.

1814 War of 1812 ends.

1817 President Madison vetoes federal funding of Erie Canal. DeWitt Clinton elected governor of New York. Famine in Ireland.

1817 July 4, state-sponsored construction of the Erie Canal begins near Rome.

1819 Completion of the 98-mile (158 km) middle section of the Erie Canal. United States in midst of economic depression after bank boom fails.

1823 First boats from completed parts of Erie Canal pass into the Hudson River.

1825 Completion of the entire Erie Canal, marked by the "Wedding of the Waters."

1826 Canal Board to administer the Erie Canal formed.

1828 DeWitt Clinton dies.

1831 First railroad in New York finished, between Albany and Schenectady.

1836 Canal expansion project started, will widen the Erie Canal to 70 feet (21.3 m), and bring the depth to 7 feet (2.1 m), allowing for more larger canalboats.

1862 Canal expansion project finished.

Glossary

appropriate The act of setting money aside for an identified purpose, as by government officials for funding government business.

aqueduct A structure that looks like a bridge and that is used to carry water over a valley.

bond (finance) A certificate issued by the government promising to repay borrowed money with interest.

boom (business/industry) To grow or expand suddenly.

bucktail A term used to describe a group of politicians in New York that opposed the Federalist party.

canalboat A long, narrow boat used on a canal with a large freight capacity.

causeway A raised road or path that goes across wet ground or water.

civil engineer An engineer who specializes in the planning and construction of public works projects, such as canals or roads.

colony An area that is controlled by or belongs to a country that is usually far away from it.

confluence A place where two rivers join and become one.

corduroy road A road built with sand-covered logs laid perpendicularly over swampy terrain to provide additional traction.

culvert A drain or pipe under a road, canal, or railway that allows water to flow under.

customhouse A building where merchants pay customs on their cargo and ships are documented.

derrick A crane-like machine used to move heavy objects.

embankment A raised bank or wall, such as a levee, built to protect an area from water.

escarpment A long cliff or steep slope that separates two flat or slightly sloped areas.

frigate A small and fast military ship.

gorge A narrow part of a steep canyon.

Haudenosaunee Also known as the Iroquois (which is sometimes considered a derogatory term), a historically powerful and important northeast Native American confederacy.

hydraulic cement A kind of cement that hardens under water, and is not very water soluble once hardened.

inflation A continual increase in the price of goods and services.

limestone A type of rock formed from compacted organic remains, such as shells or coral, that is widely used in construction.

liquidate To sell (a business, property, etc.), especially to pay off debt.

lock (canal) A device used to raise or lower boats from two different water levels whereby two gates at either end are closed and the water level is adjusted to correspond with that on the other side.

malaria A sometimes fatal disease that causes chills and fever and that is passed from one person to another by a mosquito bite.

meander A turn or winding of a stream.

navigable Deep and wide enough for boats and ships to travel on or through.

orator A person who makes speeches and is very good at making them.

piling A column made of sturdy material that is driven vertically into the ground to provide support.

portage To carry boats overland to either avoid a hazard, such as a waterfall, or to reach a different body of water.

revenue Money that is collected for public use by a government through taxes, or money that is made by or paid to a business or an organization.

sluicegate A manmade channel used to regulate the flow of water through gates or valves.

symposium A meeting where experts give their opinions on a certain topic.

tariff A tax on goods coming into or leaving a country.

terminus The end point of a transportation route.

towpath A path, such as along the shore of a canal, where draft animals tow a boat.

tributary A river or stream that flows into a larger river or lake.

weighlock A lock (as on a canal) in which boats are weighed.

Further Information

Books

Bernstein, Peter L. *Wedding of the Waters: The Erie Canal and the Making of a Great Nation.* New York: W.W. Norton & Company, 2005.

Cornog, Evan. *The Birth of Empire: DeWitt Clinton and the American Experience, 1769–1828.* New York: Oxford University Press, 1998.

Sheriff, Carol. *The Artificial River: The Erie Canal and the Paradox of Progress, 1817–1862.* New York: Hill and Wang, 1996.

Websites

The Erie Canal

www.eriecanal.org

An amazing collection of information from historical documents and maps to songs, and recommendations of books and videos on the canal.

New York State Canal Corporation

www.canals.ny.gov

News and real-time information about the current canal, as well as historical information about the canal's construction, routes, and boats.

Erie Canalway National Heritage Corridor

www.eriecanalway.org

The Erie Canalway National Heritage Corridor includes the Erie Canal and the many communities that grew up alongside it. This website includes information on a variety of topics about these areas, as well as tips on planning a trip, articles on the history of the canal, and a photo gallery.

Museums and Tours

The Erie Canal Museum

eriecanalmuseum.org

The Erie Canal Museum, located in Syracuse, New York, occupies the only existing weighlock building in America. Its website includes sections on museum news, the history of the canal, and related links.

Lockport Locks & Erie Canal Cruises

www.lockportlocks.com

The Erie Canal cruise out of Lockport, New York, is a two-hour experience that includes "locking through" the canal's only double set of locks, designed to raise boats 49 feet (15 m) to pass over the Niagara Escarpment. Each tour's boat captain shares information about the canal, Lockport, and local legends along the way.

Lockport Cave and Underground Boat Ride

lockportcave.com

Explore the secret history of the Erie Canal with a guided tour through the underground caves and the canal's manmade drainage system beneath the town of Lockport. History buffs, gear heads, and thrill seekers alike will find something to enjoy on this tour beneath the canal.

Bibliography

Adams, Samuel Hopkins. *The Erie Canal.* New York: Random House, 1953.

Andrist, Ralph K. *The Erie Canal.* New York: American Heritage Publishing Co., 1964.

Bernstein, Peter L. *Wedding of the Waters: The Erie Canal and the Making of a Great Nation.* New York: W.W. Norton & Company, 2005.

Bobbé, Dorothie. *DeWitt Clinton.* New York: Ira J. Friedman, Inc., 1962.

Bourne, Russell. *Floating West: The Erie & Other American Canals.* New York: W.W. Norton & Company, 1992.

Campbell, William W. *The Life and Writings of DeWitt Clinton.* New York: Baker and Scribner, 1849.

Chernow, Barbara Ann. *Robert Morris, Land Speculator, 1790–1801.* New York: Arno, 1978.

Condon, George E. *Stars In The Water: The Story of the Erie Canal.* New York: Doubleday & Company, Inc., 1974.

Cornog, Evan. *The Birth of Empire: DeWitt Clinton and the American Experience, 1769–1828.* New York: Oxford University Press, 1998.

Dunbar, Seymour. *A History of Travel in America: Showing the Development of Travel and Transportation from the Crude Methods of the Canoe and the Dog-sled to the Highly Organized Railway Systems of the Present, Together with a Narrative of the Human Experiences and Changing Social Conditions that Accompanied this Economic Conquest of the Continent, Volume 4.* Indianapolis; IN: Bobbs-Merrill Company, 1915.

Dunwell, Frances F. *The Hudson: America's River.* New York: Columbia University Press, 2008.

Gallatin, Albert. *Report of the Secretary of the Treasury on the Subject of Public Roads and Canals.* New York: Augustus Kelley, 1968.

Garrity, Richard G. *Canal Boatman: My Life on Upstate Waterways.* Syracuse, NY: Syracuse University Press, 1977.

———. *Recollections of the Erie Canal.* Tonawanda, NY: Historical Society of the Tonawandas, Inc., 1971.

Goetzman, William H., and Glyndwr Williams. *The Atlas of North American Exploration: From the Norse Voyages to the Race to the Pole.* New York: Macmillan General Reference, 1992.

Haines, Charles Glidden. *Considerations on the Great Western Canal from the Hudson to Lake Erie.* New York: Spooner & Worthington, 1818.

Hecht, Roger W. *The Erie Canal Reader 1790–1950.* Syracuse, NY: Syracuse University Press, 2003.

Hendrick, Welland. *A Brief History of the Empire State for Schools and Families, 3rd ed.* Syracuse, NY: C.W. Bardeen, 1895.

Hosack, David. *Memoir of DeWitt Clinton: With Appendix, Containing Numerous Documents, Illustrative of the Principal Events of His Life.* New York: J. Seymour, 1829.

Houghton, Frederick. *The Seneca Nation from 1655 to 1687.* Buffalo Society of Natural Sciences, 1912.

Klees, Emerson. *The Erie Canal in the Finger Lakes Region: The Heart of New York State.* New York: Finger Lakes Publishing, 1996.

Larkin, F. Daniel. *New York State Canals*. New York: Purple Mountain Press, 1998.

Masur, Louis P. *1831: Year of Eclipse*. New York: Hill and Wang, 2001.

McFee, Michele A. *A Long Haul: The Story of the New York State Barge Canal*. New York: Purple Mountain Press, 1999.

Morganstein, Martin, and Joan H. Cregg. *Images of America: Erie Canal*. New York: Arcadia Publishing, 2002.

Murphy, Dan. *The Erie Canal: The Ditch that Opened a Nation*. New York: Western New York Wares Inc., 2001.

Shaw, Ronald E. *Canals for a Nation: The Canal Era in the United States, 1790–1860*. Lexington, KY: University of Kentucky Press, 1990.

Shaw, Ronald E. *Erie Water West: A History of the Erie Canal, 1792–1854*. Lexington, KY: University of Kentucky Press, 1966.

Sheriff, Carol. *The Artificial River: The Erie Canal and the Paradox of Progress, 1817–1862*. New York: Hill and Wang, 1996.

United States. Congress. *Congressional Record: Proceedings and Debates of the ... Congress, Volume 13, Part 7*. US Government Printing Office, United States, 1882.

United States. Congress. House. *House Documents, Otherwise Publ. as Executive Documents: 13th Congress, 2nd Session-49th Congress, 1st Session, Volume 20: Appendix 72, The Canals of the State of New York*, pp403–500. US Government Printing Office, United States, 1885.

Van Buren, Martin. *The Autobiography of Martin Van Buren*. John Fitzpatrick, ed. Washington, DC: Government Printing Office, 1920.

Watson, Elkanah. *The Expedition*. 1792. http://www.nysm.nysed.gov/research_collections/research/history/three/bat6.html.

Whitford, Noble E. *History of the Canal System of the State of New York Together with Brief Histories of the Canals of the United States and Canada*. Albany, NY: Brandow, 1905.

Williams, Sherman. *Stories from Early New York History*. New York: C. Scribner's sons, 1906.

Index

Page numbers in **boldface** are illustrations. Entries in **boldface** are glossary terms.

About the Author

Hex Kleinmartin, PhD, has taught anthropology, archaeology, and history, worked on many archaeological excavations, and undertaken a number of instances of historical research. He has written several books and papers on subjects ranging from archaeological site reports and specialized analyses of archaeological items found on them, to the brief histories of states and their important figures. He enjoys both teaching and learning, and tries to do plenty of both with an anthropological view to help keep things in context.